BROTHER

WOLF

The Wolf of Gubbio
A Story of Saint Francis

ROBYN L STACEY

DEDICATION

God has bestowed on us
Warm fuzzy gifts from above;
Pets of all sizes and shapes –
Four-legged bundles of love.
excerpt from the poem
Blessings from Above written by Robyn L Stacey

To all the critters who have been Blessings from Above.
I love all y'all, now and forever.

CONTENTS

ACKNOWLEDGMENTS

Special thanks to God for His love, blessings and mercy.

Thank you, God, for all the dogs, cats, rabbits, etc. you have bestowed on me to care for and share this life with.

Cover Photo: A picture is worth a 1000 words; so, they say. Brother Wolf is a story of God, St Francis, a wolf, a town and forgiveness. To me, the darkness in the image represents the world without God. In the center is Light. Light is God. The one spot on the ground where the sun reflects off the water on the ground making a starburst of light is representative of God being the Light in our darkness. The white wolf is, again, representative of God's mercy & forgiveness. "..saith the Lord: if your sins be as scarlet, they shall be made as white as snow..." Isaiah 1:18.

CHAPTER 1
ANIMALS HONOR SAINT FRANCIS

Every year, on October 4th, animals around the world honor a humble man dressed in a brown robe. He was known to the animals as Brother Francis. To us, he is more widely known as Saint Francis of Assisi. He spread the Word of God while sharing God's love with all those he came in contact with.

It is said, if one could venture out to the most quiet places where wildlife wander, where city critters congregate, up in the trees where the birds of the air flock, you can hear them recite the prayer Saint Francis taught them:

"Lord, make me an instrument of Your peace;
Where there is hatred, let me sow love;
Where there is injury, pardon;
Where there is doubt, faith;
Where there is despair, hope;
Where there is darkness, light;
And where there is sadness, joy.

O Divine Master,
Grant that I may not so much seek
To be consoled as to console;
To be understood, as to understand;
To be loved, as to love;
For it is in giving that we receive,
It is in pardoning that we are pardoned,
And it is in dying that we are born to Eternal
Life.   Amen."

After praying the prayer Saint Francis taught them, they tell stories of Saint Francis. The stories have been passed from generation to generation throughout the animal kingdom for centuries.

It is said, animals watched over Saint Francis as he lay ill. They watched over him as he died. Shortly after his death, the animals began to gather to honor Saint Francis.

It is believed, before Saint Francis went on to heaven, he stayed for a time at the Rainbow Bridge comforting those animals that he knew on earth and those who had passed before their beloved owners to reassure them they would not be separated from their beloved masters forever. He visited with those who were once stray, who never knew the love of a human companion, who became stars at night guiding other strays throughout the night comforting them letting them know they, too, are still loved by God.

The older, wiser critters would retell these stories, originally told by those animals who once knew Saint Francis, to wide-eyed youngins. Mouths gaping in awe of a man they instinctively know and love in spirit.

One of these stories is the story of Saint Francis and the wolf of Gubbio, Italy. In each gathering, an older member of the group would step forward and recount the story of Brother Wolf as he once did.

Chapter 2
Brother Wolf's Story

Gather 'round, brother and sister critters!

I am a great wolf. I have hunted with my pack. I have hunted alone as a lone wolf. I am the top of my species. I am at the top of the food chain. I am a hunter. No, I am a great hunter. There was a time when I could take down a large buck with my pack, but sometimes life doesn't go the way you want it to. I found myself on my own. No pack. No hunting group. No food.

In Isaiah 11:6, it says, "the wolf shall dwell with the lamb." Before I met Brother Francis, I would have said this is true, as the

lamb makes a great meal. Brother Francis helped me realize *that* was *not* what the Book of Isaiah meant.

Not too long ago, as I said, I was separated from my pack. I became a lone wolf. It's not easy. Feels like the whole world is against you. I had to learn to do things for myself. I'm a wolf. No one's going to care about *me*... or so I thought.

I found myself wandering the countryside looking for easy prey. One day, a village lay before me.

Gubbio, Italy.

Now, this was a prosperous town of the usual townsfolk and... sheepherders. Sheepherders meant sheep were nearby... meant food for my hungry belly. I studied the little village. I watched its inhabitants. I learned their habits. Feeding schedules. Each day, the same routine. Up at dawn, feed and water the flock before they tend to crops, laundry, fence fixin', trips into town. Sometimes, they would move the flock from one pasture to another. Later in the day, often just before dark, they, once again, would feed and water the flock. Some would gather their flock and corral them into a smaller fenced area. From a hill, out of sight, I watched my quarry. No one suspected the danger that lurked in the darkness.

After many days of watching and learning, I decided it was time to make my move. In the dark of night, I quietly made my way to the fields of the shepherds. There, to my heart's delight, were the sheep I had waited for and watched from afar. I walked among them, quietly. I carefully chose one I knew I could catch. My stealth and being light on feet were always my best attributes. I descended on the flock, made my selection and took my prey to a secluded location before the missing sheep could be detected by the shepherd.

The next day, I could see the shepherd search for his missing sheep. He looked around to no avail. His eyes glanced in my direction, but I lay low in the grass. The shepherd knew nothing of my existence. With one more glance around, he shook his head and headed back to the house.

The ritual of my hunt continued for some time. Weeks went by as I kept myself well fed on the sheep of the town of Gubbio.

One night, as I crouched quietly in the grass, I slowly crept towards the town. I was intent on watching a sheep I selected from a flock. The routine became just that… routine. The "hunt" for sheep had become too easy. I let my guard down. I wasn't surveying the hunting ground for potential threats. I had no idea the villagers decided to figure out what was happening to their disappearing sheep. I didn't see the teenage boy who was intently watching me. As I watched the sheep, he hollered at me. Startled, I crouched down deeper into the grass trying to stay out of sight. He started running toward me with something in his hand. He was screaming and waving his arms about. Behind him, there was another fella, also running and shouting at me.

What could I do? I was hungry. I couldn't let these two fellas scare me away from my prey. I remained crouched in the grass. I didn't even flinch. I watched. I waited. I had made my decision. As they drew closer, I leapt from my spot in the tall grass. I headed straight for them. There was no turning back. My feet felt as though they barely touched the ground as they carried me across the pasture.

When our paths crossed, one threw a pitchfork at me. He missed, but it was close. My powerful hind legs thrust me far enough in a single bound to take them both down. We struggled. They fought with all their might, but mine was stronger.

No sooner I finished with the two lads, the figure of a man suddenly caught my attention. Once again, I failed to see danger coming at me. Everything happened so fast. He was quickly coming in my direction, screaming at the top of his lungs, flailing his arms. Fearing he, too, wanted to hurt me, I sprang to my feet. I ran straight for him. Although I was drained from the previous battle with the two boys, he was no match for me and my might. My adrenaline carried me through what I needed to do to defend myself. When all was done, I lay in the grass. It seemed like an eternity. The still of the night returned. I waited for a moment, making sure no one else came. I checked for an escape route, a quick route back to the hills and woods from whence I came. I left quickly after the encounter. For eternity was, actually, just mere moments. I had to be careful. You never know who else might have come or how many. I figured I should leave just in case. I decided: live another day to hunt again.

Chapter 3
Village Decision

I rested a few days licking my wounds.

Soon afterwards, the town gathered for a meeting. The topic of discussion was me. What to do about me. *Me?* I was minding my own business until those kids attacked me!

I secretly passed through the shadows of town. Hidden. I continued to stalk my prey. As I approached one pasture where several dogs had gathered, I heard the town dogs relating their masters' orders and stories. "Stay vigilant," they were told, "and protect the town from the wolf." *Me?* Protect against *me?* I hadn't done anything but defend myself!

The dogs said the wife of the man I killed that night a few days ago went into town with her children crying, "a wolf has killed my husband and two sons." I was sure she was just being a little overly dramatic. I mean, she had to know they threatened me. They were carrying weapons. I had no weapons. I did what any wolf would do.

While I lurked in the shadows, I tried to stay out of sight and scent of the town dogs. They actually seemed to be too involved in their conversation to even be aware of me, though. All the chatter began to bother the already on-edge townsfolk. Several yelled out of windows to the dogs to quiet down and stop all the barking. Some even came to the windows holding candlesticks to see what all the commotion was about. I guess they figured the barking wasn't anything important because they continued to yell at the dogs to shut up and some even threw things in their direction. Before the dogs quieted down, I heard them say the townspeople were going to send hunters into the woods after me to kill me. *Kill me?* What'd I do? I must remind you; I was defending myself. That man and his sons came running at me ready to hurt or kill me!

CHAPTER 4
HUNTER HUNTED

Dusk began to settle in. Those dogs were right. The hunters came right into the woods. Brave fellas I *will* say. I saw them. They each had a sword. The fading light caught each sharp blade casting a glare I could barely look at. I decided to make a quick get away.

I dashed through the underbrush in the opposite direction. The moon was full and already rising fast. Its brilliant glare shone down through the treetops. It lit my path, but it also lit me. They saw me and charged me with their swords. I darted in another direction, but another came around to block my path. I spun as fast as I could to head off in another direction. As I rushed to turn, I realized I was surrounded. I turned attempting to face each of them. I growled at them, raising my lips, hoping to scare them off. It was a ferocious growl worthy of a wolf pack alpha. They didn't scare easy.

One of them charged forward slicing with

his sword. I felt it cut through my shoulder. I caught a glimpse of the shiny blade dripping in bright red blood. I grimaced trying to control the agonizing pain. I heard a faint yelp. It seemed in the distance; yet, the voice was oddly familiar. While I attempted to stand my ground, I realized the voice I heard was mine.

I knew I couldn't let my bleeding shoulder affect me. Not now. I looked up; my face in a twisted growl. Another hunter came after me, but I got the jump on him... literally. With my claws and fangs, I swiped and bit. With my powerful front paws, I grasped him and took him down. As I turned back around, a third hunter approached me. He must have seen the other hunter succeed in taking a swipe at me. I saw the glimmer of the moon hit his sword when he swiped it at me. He missed. I lunged at him. Needless to say, my aim was better than his. I left him lying on the ground while I turned my attention to the one that sliced my shoulder.

The hunter that struck me in the shoulder watched, horrified, as I quickly took down the other two hunters. Fear emblazoned on his face; his body was frozen in terror. I thought "this will be easy." I was wrong. He somehow came to his senses. I started in his direction. He hollered to the fourth hunter. He and the fourth hunter took off running back in the direction of town. I wasn't giving up. I had them on the run. I chased them. Fortunately for them, they cleared the woods. When I reached the edge of the woods, I decided to let them go. The last I saw of the two remaining hunters was when they entered the gates of Gubbio. I

never did get the one that sliced my
shoulder.

I limped back to the safety of the woods.
My shoulder ached. I laid down on a soft
patch of earth beneath a large tree. The top
of the tree shadowed me from the glow of
the moon. Just to remind the townspeople
they had not beat me, I let out the strongest
howl I could muster.

After a couple days of rest, I waited for
the dark of night. I crept back to the
outskirts of town where the pastures of
sheep lay before me. I waited and watched. I
had to be sure it was safe. I was hungry. I
hadn't had a meal since before the battle
with the hunters. There it was. A lamb far
enough away from its mother I could snatch
it without causing much alarm. At least far
enough away I would have a good enough head
start to get away. I began to stalk placing
each foot cautiously one in front of the
other.

While I was stalking my prize, I came
face to face with one of the town dogs. His
eyes glared at me. He rolled his lips into the
nastiest snarl his domestication could afford
him. Through his teeth, dripping in all his

ferocity, he informed me of the latest efforts of the townspeople to rid the town of me. "They have sent for Brother Francis," he growled at me. Another dog came up behind me. "You'll regret you ever messed with Gubbio!" the other dog hissed. I decided, since I was injured, I did not need to battle these two huffing hounds and any townsfolk that happen to hear the commotion. Not that I couldn't take them both. I figured, if the townsfolk had sent for this Brother Francis, I may need to save my strength. I didn't need any more injuries. Like I said, my shoulder was still aching from that sword swipe. I skulked out from between the two as they continued to growl and move towards me. When clear, I ran back to the safety of my woods.

CHAPTER 5
BROTHER FRANCIS

"Brother Francis," I pondered out loud, as I walked through the woods, "hmpf! Who is this Brother Francis? What do they expect *him* to do to *me*? I am a wolf."

"He can talk to the animals," came a chorus of voices from above, high in the trees.

"Who said that?" I asked, looking up.

"We did," a flock of birds called down to me, as they fluttered their wings.
I asked the birds, "this Brother Francis can talk to animals?" I laughed out loud at the thought of some pathetic human trying to talk to animals. "How foolish you all are!

Humans cannot talk to animals." I exclaimed to the birds.

"You will see," the choir of birds taunted me in their annoying sing song way.

I will see? No, *you* will see! Foolish birds. Humans talking to animals. I snickered to myself at the very thought. *This* I am curious to see.

Early the next morning, I sat at the edge of the woods watching the gates of the village. I wondered what to expect from this "Brother Francis." I envisioned this great warrior. Big and tall. Covered in the best armor. Two very sharp, shiny swords capable of splitting hairs. A good knife and a shield to protect him from my powerful paws and jaws. Then, I chuckled to myself as I remembered the birds' declaration that this "Brother Francis" could speak to the animals.

As I imagined what Brother Francis would be like, I spied a man, frocked in brown. He was speaking with some folks at the gates of Gubbio. I studied the men for a few moments. The strange man's demeanor was not what I expected of this great Brother Francis. It couldn't possibly be him. The way the dogs spoke of him and how the townsfolk revered him he had to be some great man of war. This? This was not a man of war. This was an unassuming man dressed in simple clothes. No armor. No weapons. Nothing.

When the men appeared to be done speaking, the men of Gubbio walked back through the gate to the safety of their walls. The stranger appeared to bid them farewell

and started up the hill in the direction of my woods. I stood up. I backed up slightly, maybe a step or two, when I realized, it's *my* woods. I decided I'm not backing down to this unarmed man. I will stand my ground. I stood in perfect wolf form. A formidable beast. Predator.

The man casually strolled up the hill. He obviously saw me standing there; yet, he showed no apparent fear. His confidence bewildered me. How can this be? An unafraid human? He continued to approach until he stood just feet before me.

I hunched my back. I bristled my hair. I raised my lips. I bared my teeth. I snarled at him. All that would've been enough to scare any human into a mad dash back to the village. Not this man. He stood there. He did not budge. Stranger yet, there was a Light which seemed to radiate from him. I've never seen anything like it. It was mesmerizing, disorienting, yet, peaceful.

In a fluid motion, the man raised his hand and gestured to his head, his chest, then, his left shoulder and his right while declaring these words, "In the name of the Father, and of the Son, and of the Holy Ghost." He then lowered his hand and spoke to me.

"Come, Brother Wolf, I will not hurt you," the man addressed me with a calm voice while holding his hand out toward me. I took advantage, and I sniffed his hand. He smiled at me and said, "Be not afraid, Brother Wolf. Let us talk."

I did not understand why this man had such power over me. His mere presence calmed all my anxieties towards humans. Last, but definitely not least, I understood him. I understood the words he spoke. How is it that I, a wolf, could understand him, a human? Humans cannot speak to animals. Wolves cannot speak to humans. How is this possible? Baffled and confused; I agreed to speak with him.

He ushered me to the shade of an olive tree, and he sat on the ground beside me. He did not hover over me. He got down on my level. He presented himself as my equal. I was tempted to pull the alpha wolf on him, but something about him made me choose not to.

"My name is Francis," he gently offered, "what is your name?"

"I am a lone wolf. I have no name," I responded. "Why would I have a name?" I explained there was no one who cared about me to give me a name. "A name is for those who are cared about. No one cares about me. I am hated by humans. The only names I have hurled at me are curse words."

With a concerned look upon his face, Francis said to me, "in Luke 12:7, it says, 'the very hairs of your head are all numbered.' Do you know what this means?"

"No," I answered gazing back down the hill at Gubbio.

"It means *God knows* you, *cares* for you and *loves* you. You are *His* creation, just as *all* the other animals of the woods are His creation. Even the trees providing us this glorious shade from the heat of the sun, He knows the number of leaves each has."

CHAPTER 6
FRANCIS SPEAKS OF GOD

Francis continued to speak to me of God all morning. I listened intently. I was in awe of such a Being. Francis told me how God got angry at the sins of man a long time ago. He instructed Noah to build an Ark to save the animals. Even then, God loved all His creations as to not let them all suffer. His mercy was endless. Francis told me among the animals Noah took aboard the Ark was my ancestors. Wolves. His mercy saved wolves like me from a massive flood that destroyed everything. I can't even imagine so much rain to flood the earth.

Francis began to tell me how the people of Gubbio were hurt by what I did. He said I killed five of their loved ones. He explained to me how humans were made in the image of

God. I was amazed at this God and what Brother Francis told me. He explained he wanted to bring peace to the people of Gubbio and me. He wanted a solution to our problem; so, we would not go on hating and killing each other.

I explained to Francis I was a lone wolf. I do not have a pack to hunt with. Being a lone wolf, I have to find food where I can. The sheep were easy for me to hunt by myself. I told him I would much rather hunt with my pack, but they were long gone. I had to survive. Hunting smaller prey or the humans' sheep was the best I could do. I never hurt the humans. I only hunted the sheep. Why couldn't they share their sheep? They had so many. I never meant the humans any harm, but they came running after me with weapons. I feared they would hurt me or worse, kill me. I did what I thought I had to do to protect myself. When they sent hunters after me, they set out to kill me. You could not fault me for trying to protect myself.

I asked him, "You say your God cares for me and loves me, but does he want me to be hungry or die?"

To my surprise, Francis listened to my story. I showed him the wound on my shoulder from the hunter's sword. It was still raw and festering. Francis looked at the wound, and he cleaned it.

He smiled at me again and told me, "it is true. You, too, need to eat and survive, but you cannot attack the people of Gubbio. God *does* love you and care for you; so, we will have to pray for a solution to this situation."

I watched as Francis became very quiet. He knelt in the grass with his head bowed, and folded his hands together. As I sat beside him, he prayed. He asked God to help us find a solution to this problem; one we all could live with.

While Francis prayed, I felt a warm, gentle peace fill my heart and soul. When Francis said "Amen", he opened his eyes. He looked into mine as I sat before him. He smiled at me and said, "Come, Brother Wolf, God has spoken to me." With those words, he stood, motioned to me to follow, and, together, we walked toward the gates of Gubbio. Francis told me what God said to him while we walked down the hill to Gubbio.

Upon entering the gates, Francis and I walked side by side; the townspeople gasped. Their eyes fixated on me. Glaring at me. I started to slow my gait, lowered my head and tail, as their stares pierced my soul. Francis stopped walking until my slow gait caught up with him. He placed his hand on my head. "Stay beside me, Brother Wolf," Francis reassured me.

Some of the people of Gubbio started to walk briskly away. "Stop!" Francis ordered them. "He means you no harm," he explained as he pointed in my direction.

The people stopped and slowly made their way back to where we were standing.

"You must work together for peace between you. I have a solution, but you all must agree," Francis addressed the townspeople. "Brother Wolf has agreed to no longer terrorize the town or harm its people. But, in return, you, the townspeople, must agree to care for him and feed him. He has agreed to be your protector... your guardian."

The people began to mutter amongst themselves. "How can this be?" Why would he want to protect us?" They continued to question the words of Brother Francis.

Finally, to show everyone we meant what Francis had said, Francis offered me, once again, his hand. I was sitting beside him. This time, instead of sniffing it, I placed my paw in his hand. We shook to seal the agreement.

The townsfolk began to murmur, "It's a miracle!"

Francis began to preach to the people about the forgiveness of our enemies' sins in order to have our own sins forgiven. He quoted Scriptures written long ago to make his point. He reminded them hatred was a heavy burden which separated us from God. Finally, Francis asked them if they would forgive me and accept the agreement for peace.

The townsfolk responded "yes" in unison, as they nodded their heads in approval.

In an ultimate gesture of forgiveness, the widow of the man I killed emerged from the crowd. In her hands, she carried a warm dish with an evening meal. She placed the dish at my feet and said, "I forgive you, Brother Wolf."

As I gratefully finished the meal, the crowd began to come forward. They thanked Francis and offered me their hands in peace and friendship. I placed my paw in each of their hands.

Soon, it was time for Francis to leave. I walked with him out of the gates of Gubbio. We walked to the other side of the woods. I protected him from danger and provided him safe passage. He shared with me more of the Wisdom of God. Before he left, Francis

turned to me, bent down on one knee and said, "You see, Brother Wolf, God *does* care about you and loves you. With prayer, He has given us a solution that benefits both you and the people of Gubbio."

I licked his hand and he wrapped an arm around my neck. He whispered into my ear, "and now you have a name, Brother Wolf."

Brother Francis stood up, patted me on the head and left on his journey back to Assisi.

CHAPTER 7
LEGACY

With Francis' blessing, I share my story with each of you, my fellow brother and sister critters. I ask you to forgive those who have done you harm or mean you harm; for it is written, "the wolf shall dwell with the lamb." I have learned through Brother Francis that Isaiah did not mean the lamb makes a great meal. Isaiah meant two opposites, prey and predator, will live together in peace. That the Lamb of God will bring peace to all.

I held true to my part of the agreement, and the people of Gubbio held to their part of the agreement. I protected them from all outside dangers. They fed me and cared for me for the rest of my life. The widow and her children forgave me. Many nights I spent lying outside their home guarding against intruders and other wild things. I felt it was the least I could do. She would sneak me special treats.

I helped the dogs guard against other wild animals. I taught them how to lie in silence. They taught me how to play. We lived together and we learned from each other.

"This was the story of Brother Francis and Brother Wolf," the animal elders concluded their story. Brother Francis visited Gubbio several times. Brother Wolf was always glad to see Brother Francis. He learned to wag his tail and he held his head high. When Francis approached, Brother Wolf offered his paw. Brother Francis always greeted his friend by shaking his paw. Brother Wolf lived with the townsfolk of Gubbio, Italy for a few more years. They fed and cared for him, and he guarded the village until his death of old age. Through this story being passed down through the animals, through the descendants of Gubbio and those that knew Brother Francis, he and Brother Wolf will always be remembered.

The legacy of Brother Francis and Brother Wolf is forgiveness and mercy. The legacy of Brother Francis and Brother Wolf is peace. The legacy of Brother Francis and Brother Wolf is no matter who you are, great or small, prey or predator, God loves you.

"Bearing with one another, and forgiving one another, if any have a complaint against another: even as the Lord hath forgiven you, so do you also." Colossians 3:13

"Forgive, I beseech thee, the sins of this people, according to the greatness of thy mercy." Numbers 14:19

"Are not five sparrows sold for two farthings, and not one of them is forgotten before God? Yea, the very hairs of your head are all numbered. Fear not." Luke 12:6-7

"In God I trust. I shall not be afraid." Psalm 56:11

"Be strong and of good courage. Fear not and be not dismayed. The Lord your God is with you in all things wherever you shall go." Joshua 1:9

ABOUT THE AUTHOR

Robyn Stacey is an animal caretaker/rescuer, photographer, graphic designer, genealogist and writer. She inherited her love of animals from her mom and her interest in photography from her dad & maternal grandma. Robyn became interested in genealogy at the young age of at least 10 years old thanks to her dad's interest in the history of his father's family. Robyn is a proud United States Air Force brat and native Texan.

Quotes:
"My hope is for folks to see beyond the man-made world and, instead, see the beautiful world God has bestowed upon us!"
"Pawsing for Critters with Four Paws!"

Robyn's photography & Paws4Critters graphic design line can be purchased around the internet at:

robyn-stacey.pixels.com
www.robynstaceyphotos.etsy.com
www.cafepress.com/paws4critters
www.cafepress.com/americausa

Robyn has the following books published and available for purchase on Amazon.
Mama, Where Do Strays Go?
Colorful Cats Adult Grayscale Coloring Book
Classic Cars Adult Grayscale Coloring Book
Orphaned By War The Stacy Saga

Follow Robyn's photography, graphic design and books on Facebook at
www.facebook.com/robynstaceypaws4crittersphotography
or her blog at http://paws4critters.blog

Made in the USA
Middletown, DE
13 November 2020